Anima the Rainforest

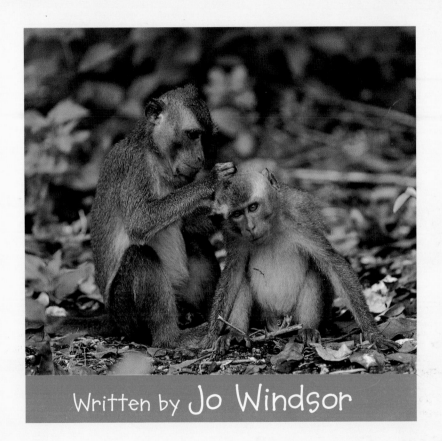

Written by Jo Windsor

Rigby

Parrots are
in the rainforest.

3

Elephants are
in the rainforest.

Monkeys are in the rainforest.

Frogs are in the rainforest.

9

Butterflies are
in the rainforest.

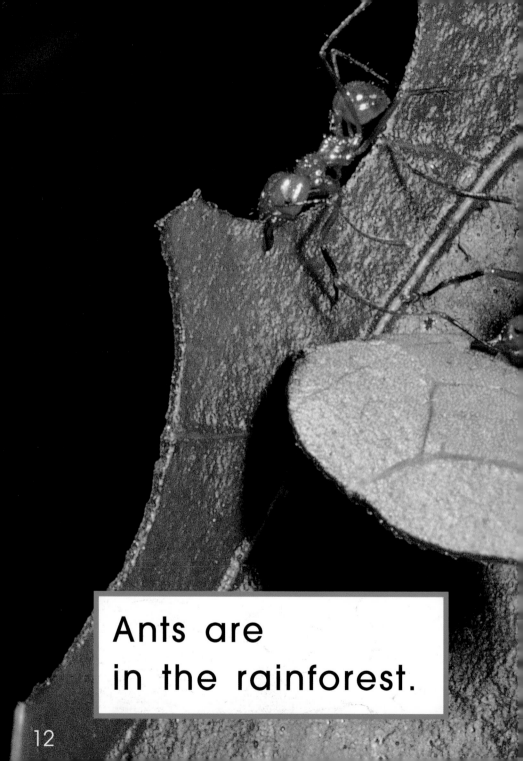

Ants are
in the rainforest.

13

Index

▬▬▬ **Guide Notes**

Title: Animals of the Rainforest
Stage: Emergent – Magenta

Genre: Nonfiction (Expository)
Approach: Guided Reading
Processes: Thinking Critically, Exploring Language, Processing Information
Written and Visual Focus: Photographs (static images), Illustrations, Index
Word Count: 30

READING THE TEXT

Tell the children that this book is about some animals that live in the rainforest.
Talk to them about what is on the front cover. Read the title and the author.
Focus the children's attention on the index and talk about the animals that are in this book.
"Walk" through the book, focusing on the photographs and talk about the different animals that live in the rainforest.
Read the text together.

THINKING CRITICALLY
(sample questions)
• What other animals live in the rainforest?
• What would it be like living in the rainforest?

EXPLORING LANGUAGE
(ideas for selection)

Terminology
Title, cover, author, photographs, illustrations

Vocabulary
Interest words: rainforest, ants, butterflies, elephant, frog, monkey, parrot
High-frequency words: are, in, the